The Women of Judges

John Sawyer

Parson's Porch Books
www.parsonsporchbooks.com

The Women of Judges
ISBN: Softcover 978-1-949888-65-2
Copyright © 2018 by John Sawyer

All rights reserved. No part of this book may be reproduced or transmitted in any form or by any means, electronic or mechanical, including photocopying, recording, or by any information storage and retrieval system, without permission in writing from the publisher.

The Women of Judges

Contents

Preface 7
Introduction 9
Acsah 13
    Judges 1:1-15
Deborah 16
    Judges 4 and 5
Jael 20
    Judges 4 and 5
Mother Of Sisera 24
    Judges 5:28-30
The Woman Who Killed Abimalech 28
    Judges 8:29-9:57
Jephthah's Daughter 31
    Judges 11
Samson's Mother 35
    Judges 13
Philistine Woman Of Timnah 38
    Judges 14-15
Delilah 42
    Judges 16
Micah's Mother 46
    Judges 17
The Levite's Concubine 50
    Judges 19

Four Hundred Virgins and Two Hundred Dancing Girls 54
    Judges 17-21
Naomi 58
    Book of Ruth
Ruth 62
    Book of Ruth
Hannah 67
    I Samuel 1:1-28

Preface

The writing of *The Women of Judges* was written, as were my previous two books, through a request from Dr. Arthur Crisco. Art is the volunteer editor for a Christian missionary organization. The original request was for leaflets on eleven women in The Book of Judges in the Hebrew Bible (Old Testament). Then he suggested the material be put into a book. I edited the leaflet material and added material on each. I included a chapter on the abducted women found in the last two chapters of Judges. I also added Naomi, Ruth and Hannah who lived in the time of the Judges. The Scripture translation I use is from the New Revised Standard Version (NRSV).

The other two books mentioned above: *The Jesus Story, Musings for* Meditation and Application and *The Paul Story, Musings for Meditation and Application*. Both are available from ParsonsPorchBooks.com or through your favorite book store.

All three books were made possible through the gracious help of my wife, Eloise; the encouragement of Dr. Crisco and the publisher, Dr. David Tullock.

Introduction

To write about the women of in The Book of Judges requires a word about the times and happenings in that period, according to what is found in the book itself.

There is some information that should be known and recalled for all the studies of the women of Judges.

The *Book of Judges* is a collection of stories about the Hebrew people after the death of Joshua. Think through a quick review. Genesis tells how Jacob's family, by Joseph's powerful position in the Egyptian government was able to move from Palestine into Egypt. Exodus tells how, after the death of Joseph, the Jews became slaves of Pharaoh, and how God delivered them from slavery.

Leviticus, Numbers and Deuteronomy continue the story of their wilderness travels and major expansions and interpretation of the laws they were to live by. The

Book of Joshua tells how Moses' military leader and servant, Joshua, led in capturing the promised land, Palestine.

But the land was not totally conquered. Joshua ends with none of the twelve tribes completing the job of driving out their enemies and possessing their designated land.

So, the *Book of Judges* tells of one of the darkest times in the life of the Jews. All twelve tribes fought among themselves and with their enemies. Some of the most horrible stories told in the Bible are in Judges. There was violence, war, stealing, rape, murder, you name the evil; these stories tell it. Much of the evil was directed toward women. But, in these stories you will find women of courage, faith, strength and other qualities that enable persons to stand firm in times of adversity. There was a cycle of five events that recurred over and over in The Book of Judges. 1. There was a time of peace. 2. The people would forsake God and worship other gods. 3. Their enemies would defeat and control them. 4. They would cry out to God in repentance. 5. God would raise a judge to deliver them, giving them peace for a while. Then the cycle began again.

Judges were usually warriors. Their job was to defend their tribe from the 'pagan' enemy and sometimes from other tribes of their own people. Judges were also persons who settled disputes and made decisions for the tribe.

Here are a few helps for interpretation. It was a time of patriarchy, males were in charge and women often abused; conquest by violence; belief that God ordered violence. The Book of Judges, as with all scripture, should be interpreted in the light of Jesus' teaching and life of love, mercy, justice and nonviolent peacemaking.

Another thing to keep in mind, when your jaw drops to ask," Did they really do that?" Nothing happened then that is not happening today. Look at the world around you. Start close to home. And the frightening thing is, we all carry some responsibility. We vote for corrupt politicians. We buy products from corrupt corporations; products made by slave labor, products sold with financial gain the only aim. If we have education, a good paying job with healthcare and retirement benefits and modern conveniences; should not everyone have the opportunity for them?

There will be suggestions for serious ethical thought, discussion and action in the Application to Life section at the end of each chapter.

The purpose of the book is to help you look at yourself, your church, community and world and examine your own life.

Acsah

Judges 1:1-15

Acsah the Given Bride

Acsah was the daughter of Caleb. He was associated with Joshua as one of two of the twelve spies of Moses who gave a positive report concerning an attack against the enemy in Palestine. Read the story in Numbers 13. Caleb offered to give Acsah to the warrior who could lead in the defeat of Debir.

Othniel, Acsah's first cousin, accepted the challenge, won the battle and married Acsah. Read this same story, almost word for word in Joshua 15: 13-19. Also, read of Saul offering his daughter to David in I Samuel 18:17-28. Note the power of the father, Caleb, to give his daughter to whomever he chose. Do you think she as consulted? Othniel is listed as, perhaps the first of the Judges. See Judges 3:9-12.

Acsah the Requesting Bride

Acsah was not a timid lady. She went to her father to request a field (her dowry?). Numbers 27:1-11 tells another story that indicates it was right for a woman to make such a request. But Acsah is not satisfied with what may have been desert land and asks for another field also. She gets her request. Mark one up for Acsah and God in a male dominated society. Would you say Acsah was a bold lady in a difficult situation? Does the passage speak of Caleb's justice toward and love for his daughter?

Application to Life

Read Genesis 1:27-28. Think about and discuss with your study group: How prevalent is it for fathers or mothers to choose marriage partners for their children in your society? What about parents who insist on a child choosing from a certain economic, social, racial, political, or religious class? Should men and women have equal say about whom they marry?

A number of equal rights questions may be discussed. Acsah claimed her right to own property. Name other rights that need to be equal in your society: jobs, pay, education, religion…

Prayer: *Lord, help us accept all persons as created in your image.*

Deborah

Judges 4 and 5

Introduction

As preparation for this second study on the women in the Book of Judges, read or reread the introduction of the first study. It emphasizes that the violence in Judges must be interpreted today in the light of the nonviolent life and teaching of Jesus.

Now, read the text for this study on Deborah in Judges 4 and 5.

Notice that the story is told once in prose in chapter four and in poetry in chapter five.

Did you notice that Deborah was a judge, wife, "mother in Israel," and prophetess? No wonder her name means "bee."

She was "busy as a bee."

Another key in Bible study is to interpret according to the type or genre. Poetry uses imagination to express truth, often more than prose. In Jewish poetry, the first line is often repeated in other words in the second line.

Much scripture lends itself to various interpretations. The rabbis (teachers) are known for their questions, answers and disagreements. One is said to have asked a rabbi, "Why do you always answer a question with a question?"

The rabbi replied, "Why Not?"

Deborah the Lady

Most scholars believe "Deborah woman of Lappidoth" means that she was married to a man by that name. It is possible that it means she was from a place by that name. So, if married she was probably a mother. "Mother in Israel" could mean she had birthed a child or children, but it could mean she was famous as in George Washington called the father of the U. S. A. Whatever, she was a highly honored lady in Israel.

Deborah the Judge

As noted in the first study, judges were usually military leaders or warrior type men who rose up to fight and defeat an oppressing enemy. Deborah actually "held court" under a date palm tree that was given her name. People came to her to settle disputes. Do you think that being a wife and mother helped her understand the problems of others? Do you imagine her to be compassionate, wise and just in her decisions?

Deborah is one of the few women called a prophet. In the story her territory is threatened, and she calls on a military leader named Barak to gather an army and defeat the enemy. He agrees only if she will go with him. Don't you find that unusual? She agrees but tells him the glory of the victory will go to a woman.

In the story of the battle you might be reminded of the Egyptian army chasing Moses into the bed of the Red Sea on iron wheeled chariots (Exodus 14). Barak and Deborah overcame the enemy army because God sent a storm and flood that bogged down the chariots and the soldiers fled. Their general, Sisera, deserted his army, fled to what he thought was a safe place and was killed by a woman (as predicted by Deborah). That is a story for the next study.

Application to life

It was unusual for a woman to be a judge in a patriarchal society. What about in your society? Is there sex or gender discrimination in your government, business arena, church, home? What are your own feelings about the equality of women?

Do you ever think of God possessing feminine or motherly qualities? There are such metaphors throughout the Bible.

Why do you think most, if not all, nations of our world today still seek to solve problems with weapons of war, violence and death? How many persons or nations are willing to seek peace through listening, understanding and compassion for each other?

Consider reading *Twelve Steps to a Compassionate Life* by Karen Armstrong. and Google the Charter of Compassion.

Prayer: *Dear God, help us to be peacemakers. Amen.*

Jael
Judges 4 and 5

Introduction

Have you noticed on television news an occasional warning is given? It might say, "The material you are about to see is disturbing." Such a warning might be appropriate for the story of Jael. In fact, it could be said for the whole book of Judges. Remember, in both the first studies a suggestion was made that this book should be studied from a viewpoint of the advanced ethics of the life and teachings of Jesus, as recorded in the Gospels of Matthew, Mark, Luke and John.

The text for study three is the same as study two, Judges chapters four and five. Read the story again. Attention in this study is focused on a tent dwelling lady named Jael, wife of a Kenite named Heber. The Kenites were descendants of Moses' father-in-law. Heber was a friend of King Jabin of Hazor the enemy of Deborah's folk. Sisera, Jabin's general, who deserted his army seemed to think there was friendship and safety for him at Heber's tent. The word Jael means mountain goat. Do you think that fits the lady, Jael, who bore that name?

In the study focus on Jael's gracious hospitality and her gory human cruelty.

Jael the Hostess

As stated above, and seen twice in Judges four and five, Sisera fled the battle and came to the tent of Heber and Jael. He asked for protection, requesting that if someone came looking for him, she was to say he was not there. He also asked for water. Jael puts him to bed and brings him goat milk. The scene is touching as she seems to give tender care and hospitality that exceeded his request. Or, you may see the scene as seductive on the part of Jael. In exhaustion and fear he placed his life in her care. He soon fell asleep.

Jael the Murderer

The gracious hospitality was followed by a gory murder. It was custom that nomadic women knew how and pitched tents. Jael was familiar with tent pegs and mallets or hammers. So, she took a tent peg and while Sisera slept she drove it through his temple. Here is the poetic account from one version of 5:26-27:

She put her hand to the tent peg
and her right hand to the workman's mallet;
she struck Sisera a blow,
she crushed his head,
she shattered and pierced his temple.
He sank, he fell, he lay still at her feet;
at her feet he sank, he fell;
where he sank, there he fell dead.

Our fourth study will begin at that point in the poem. It will focus on the mother of Sisera and the sorrow of war.

Application to Life

Hospitality is taught throughout the Bible. Read and discuss with your study group the following passages Deuteronomy 10:17-19; 23:16; 24:17-22; Leviticus 19:33; Luke 10:4-9; Mark 2:13-18; Matthew 7:12 and 25:31-46.

You can find a great number of times where Jesus gave and received hospitality. Read Romans 12:13, Hebrews 13:2.

Continue your discussion about the need for peacemaking and hospitality as a means to prevent violence.

Prayer: *May we learn from Jesus to be gracious, non-violent hosts. Amen*

Mother of Sisera
Judges 5:28-30

Introduction

This is the fourth in a series of studies of women in the Book of Judges. This study deals with the emotions, both positive and negative, of the mother of a soldier. Try to imagine the emotions of family, friends or loved ones of men and women in military service and at war. Many of you already know the experience of these emotions. This study is very relevant to your society where ever you live.

It would be good to reread chapters four and five of Judges to get the setting. It will help in interpreting the short passage about Sisera's mother, 5:28-30. The mother of Sisera, the general of the enemy army, was speaking to her servants and perhaps other family members. She was looking out the window expecting the safe return of her son from a victorious battle.

She had begun to wonder why the long delay. She tried to be positive. Maybe so much loot was taken that it took extra time to divide all the material among the men. Maybe there were so many women taken captive that every man had several. They are having an orgy, she must have thought. They will bring beautiful garments to her she thought. Read the text with imagination:

"Through the window peered Sisera's mother;
behind the lattice she cried out,
'Why is the chariot so long in coming?
Why is the clatter of his chariots delayed?'
The wisest of her ladies answer her;
indeed, she keeps saying to herself,
'Are they not finding and dividing the spoils:
a girl or two for each man'
colorful garments as plunder for Sisera,
colorful garments embroidered,
highly embroidered garments for my neck
all this as plunder?'

Wishing and hoping; but tragic news was coming. Her son had been slaughtered by a woman.

Is there a family in your neighborhood not touched by the horror and grief of war? Friend or foe, "win or lose" soldiers and their families suffer physical, psychological, emotional, financial, you name it, tragedy.

Yet, supposedly civilized, societies continue to seek prestige, power and possessions through war at the cost of the lives of soldiers and civilians. It is barbaric and becomes more so with the increase in scientific ways of warfare.

How far from the peacemaking Jesus have great powers gone?

Application to Life

You and or your group may profit from a study of *The Politics of Jesus* by John Howard Yoder.

Investigate organizations that work for peace and consider what you can or should do.

Explore opportunities in your community for volunteering to help families affected by war: hospitals, rehab centers.

Find how you can help a mother whose son or husband is away in the military.

Pray for the victims of war, military and civilian, friend and foe, and corporation and governmental leaders who instigate conflicts.

Reach out to other nationalities, religions, and races to work for peace in your community.

Prayer: *Lord, teach us to be peacemakers, beginning at home.*

The Woman Who Killed Abimelech

Judges 8:29-9:57

Introduction

This is the fifth of the studies on the women in the Book of Judges. Recall the five-step cycle of events described in the first study. 1. A tribe, or tribes and possibly at times, all the tribes lived in peace. 2. Then they would follow other gods or idols, forgetting the God of Israel. 3. God would give them over to an enemy which would persecute them. 4. They would cry out to God in repentance asking for deliverance. 5. God would raise up a "judge" to deliver them and they would have peace again.

The long passages for this study, Judges 8:29 – 9:57, tells of one of those cycles. Read the passage carefully, there are lots of details and characters. Look for the five-step cycle.

One. Forty Years of Peace

Under Judge Gideon, also called Jerub Baal, Israel had forty years of peace. You may want to read that story in chapters 6-8 of Judges. Gideon was one of the great Judges. He had 70 sons and many wives. He also had one son, by a concubine, named Abimelech.

Two. Forgetting God and Gideon

No sooner had Gideon died than the people forgot what God had done for them through Gideon. Read 8:33-35.

Abimelech had probably been disinherited by them and had gone to his mother, the concubine. Upon Gideon's death he returns and kills the seventy brothers (except the youngest).

Three. Abimelech Destroyed Many People

Abimelech killed sixty-nine half-brothers. He was a cruel warrior. He burned a tower filled with citizens.

Four. An Unnamed Woman to the Rescue

All this long story to get to 9:50-54 and the unnamed woman who saved her city. Having burned one tower filled with people, Abimelech went to another city to do the same thing. But as he approached the tower, a woman cast a stone down on his head. He knew he was dying and called for his armor bearer to kill him with his sword, "so that they can't say", 'A woman killed him.'

Five. There Was Peace

Application to Life

Take your pick from the topics of application for life in an age of sexism. Should women do the same jobs as men? Should women receive equal pay for the same job? How is it where you live? Is there equal opportunity for education, jobs, pay, justice, etc.? A lot of progress has been made, but there is still a long way to go in these issues. What about in the church? Should women be treated as equal to men in religious work? Is your society bound by the rules, written or unwritten, of patriarchy? Read Genesis 1:27.

Prayer: *Thank you God for creating all human beings in your image. Amen.*

Jephthah's Daughter
Judges 11

Introduction

The stories get sadder. The unnamed, only, and virgin daughter of Jephthah gives up her life for the foolishness of her father. Read the text, Judges 11. Notice the many and varied relationships in the story. Though this study will focus on the daughter, she does not live or die in isolation.

Watch for the change in relationship of Jephthah's half-brothers to him when they need a warrior judge. See how, to his credit, Jephthah tries to make peace through discussion twice before using violence. The story centers on his relationship with his daughter; and hers with him. And finally consider her relationship to her female friends.

This study will deal with these relationships.

Jephthah and His Brothers

According to the story, Jephthah is the son of Gilead by a prostitute. For this reason, his brothers want nothing to do with him. They drove him away, sent him to his mother.

But when trouble came, and they need a warrior to deliver them they ask him to come back. He returned, gathered an army, but on the condition that if he won, he would become their permanent leader.

Jephthah and His Daughter

For some reason, before going to battle, Jephthah made a vow to God. As it turns out, a very stupid vow. He vowed that should he win the battle, he would sacrifice the first to come from his house on his return. What was he thinking? Did he think an animal would come out to meet him? As you know, it was his only daughter who came out to greet him.

Read Exodus 15:20-21 and I Samuel 18:6-7 for an idea of how singing and dancing were part of the celebration of victory. From victory shouts to tears of grief.

Read Exodus 13:13 and Leviticus 18:21 to see that human sacrifice was not acceptable. To try to understand Jephthah's dilemma read Numbers 30:3 and Deuteronomy 23:22-24.

What do you think of the daughter's attitude and words? She is willing to be sacrificed, but asks for time to mourn her virginity. As a Hebrew female, she had hope of fulfilling life by being a mother. That would never be now.

Jephthah's Daughter and Her Friends

She asked for two months to go away with friends to mourn. The story does not tell how she died. But it does say that a permanent memorial was set in place by Hebrew women to remember her.

Application to Life

Questions to consider. Who is excluded, like Jephthah, from your family? Who is excluded from your church? When does something done as a religious act become stupid? Are lives more important than promises? Do you bargain with God? "If you do this God, then I'll do that." Do you think the retreat was with her support group? Do you have a support group? What do you know about AA, Alcoholics Anonymous? It is a good example of how a support group works.

Prayer: *Lord, teach us to be wise, inclusive and supportive.*

Samson's Mother
Judges 13

Introduction

This is a study of the mother of Samson. Do you find it interesting that she is unnamed? Seven of the eleven women in the book of Judges studied in this series are not named. Samson's father is named Manoah. Should you call his mother Mrs. Manoah? She must have had a huge influence on Samson. He became a very famous character in the Hebrew Bible. Some might say infamous character.

As you read the text, Judges 13, look for the spiritual and parental qualities of the mother of Samson.

Samson's Mother Was a Spiritual Person

You can add "Mrs. Manoah" to the list of barren wives in the Hebrew Bible. Take time to review these: Sarah, wife of Abraham, Genesis 18:1-15; Rebekah, wife of

Isaac, Genesis 25:19-27; Rachel, wife of Jacob, Genesis 30:1-24; Hannah, wife of Elkhana, I Samuel 1:1-29; Woman of Shunem, I Kings 4:8-17. Do you find it interesting that barrenness was attributed to the woman? Was this a lack of genetic knowledge or a blame thing? Each of these stories gives emphasis to the power of God enabling these women to have children. So, in this study, an angel (messenger) of God comes to Mrs. Manoah to announce that she will be a mother.

Her son, Samson, is to be reared a Nazarite, see the book of Numbers chapter 6. He was not to drink strong drink or cut his hair. In Samson's case, his unusual strength is related to his uncut hair. The instructions given by the "angel" were important to Samson's mother.

Samson's Mother as a Wife and Parent

Did you note that "Mrs. Manoah" was quick to share her experience with her husband. He then wanted to have this encounter with the "angel." Did you note that on the trips to meet the women of Samson's life, his mother went with her husband? Despite their advice and guidance Samson was strong willed and had things his way. As you read of the misuse of strength by Samson, recall Jesus' way of nonviolence.

Application to Life

Discuss the fact that Samson's mother was not to drink strong drink during her pregnancy. Is that the way you read it? Up to date isn't it? What are you and your church doing to provide safe and supportive environment for expectant and new mothers? How does your church and community assist in the care and education of children?

How do your labor laws provide health insurance for lower wage earners, women and working mothers? Are there good support groups for those dealing with marriage and parental problems?

Prayer: *Lord, make us sensitive and helpful to parents and children.*

Philistine Woman of Timnah
Judges 14-15

Introduction

This study is based on tales of the famous or infamous character known as Samson. He is said to have judged Israel for twenty years. Samson, according to the story, is less a judge in the sense of Deborah (Judges 4-5) or a military leader as some of the others. And certainly, there is question about his spiritual leadership, though he was reared as a Nazirite (chapter 13).

The woman of Timnah is a pawn in the story. This study requires imagination and speculation to identify with and learn from the lady.

As you read the text, Judges 14-15, keep these questions in mind. Was Samson's attraction more lust than love? Did Samson not trust her, so he kept his riddle a secret from her for seven days? Was she treated as an "object" when given to Samson's best man? Should loyalty to "blood kin," friends (the thirty men), and country (she was a Philistine) be greater than to marriage partner?

The Woman of Timnah was an "Object"

From the beginning of the story Samson's words were "Get her for me." Does it sound as though he had her on a shopping list with horses, chariots, and clothes? "Get her for me," he told his parents. His parents tried to reason with him; that the Philistines were longtime enemies of Israel, and besides, there were beautiful Jewish girls available. But Samson wins the argument. The woman of Timnah was bargained for and a wedding was planned.

A Woman Manipulated, Manipulates

How much say do you think the bride to be had in the plans? Did she love Samson? Was she manipulated by Samson and her own father? What about the thirty men who spent the week getting her to find out Samson's riddle secret? Does she, the manipulated one, become the manipulator. She kept on till Samson gave her the secret.

The Woman was Trapped by Family, Friends and Custom

This study is not to judge nor condemn the lady. It is to try to learn from her. Can you imagine how it would be to be told you will marry a person who is a foreigner with different religious, political, and cultural beliefs? Was she not trapped between Samson and her friends? Add your questions to these as you imagine her situation.

Application to Life

How are marriages decided in your society? What freedom does the man or lady have in the decision? Do you think many marriages are based more on lust than love?

There must be openness and honesty. Add to these five areas that need to be discussed and worked out.

1. Faith. If faith or religion are different for the couple, then some mutual plans need to be decided on before marriage.

2. Finances. There needs to be a budget based on income and expense. Agreement on how the money is made and spent is necessary before marriage.

3. Family. Have children when, why, why not, etc. Extended family is part of the deal. Can you be civil toward all?

4. Friends. How do they fit in. Are they more important than should be?

5. Fun. What do you enjoy doing together?

Prayer: *Lord, help us to be the best marriage partners we can be.*

Delilah

Judges 16

Introduction

This study of the famous lady named Delilah could be called "When Romance Becomes Political." To better understand the impact of what Delilah did it would be helpful to read the full story of Samson in Judges 13-16.

Consider the number of lust/love pursuits of Samson. Notice the havoc he caused to individuals, families and towns of the Philistines. He killed thirty men of the city of Ashkelon to get thirty garments to pay his wager to the groomsmen. The story does not record how many acres of grain and vineyards he destroyed with the 300 torch bearing foxes. This was done because his father-in-law gave the wife Samson deserted to the best man in the wedding.

When his own countrymen gave him to the Philistines, he killed 3,000 of them with the jawbone of a donkey. On a visit to a prostitute in the Philistine city of Gazaan an attempt to arrest him resulted in his pulling up the posts and gates of the city. He walked off, carrying them with him.

He was addicted to Philistine women and Delilah is just the one most famous.

Delilah's Relationship was Political

The story tells that Samson fell in love with Delilah. It does not say that Delilah fell in love with Samson. Do you think he was set up? The story does not say how they met.

Did the Philistines use her to get to Samson? Is it not obvious that Samson's weakness, addiction, craving is for Philistine women? However, it happened, the Philistine leaders knew of his relationship to Delilah. "The rulers of the Philistines went to her and said, see if you can lure him into showing you the secret of his great strength and how we can overpower him so we may tie him up and subdue him.

Each one of us will give you eleven hundred shekels of silver" (Judges 16:5). Money bought her. Sound political?

Delilah was Persistent

You can hear her persistence in verses 15-16. "Then she said to him, 'How can you say, "I love you," when you don't confide in me? This is the third time you have made a fool of me and haven't told me the secret of your great strength.'

With such nagging she prodded him day after day until he was tired to death." Finally, adding tears to nagging she got what she wanted, a lot of money. Samson lost his strength and sight and became a slave to the Philistines.

Application to Life

Consider these questions for thought and discussion.

What is your addiction?

What is it that drives you?

Is there danger that you may be like Delilah?

What would you not do for money?

Discuss the addictive power of prestige, power, possessions, sex, shopping, drugs, and ….

Prayer: *God, help us to see and overcome our addictions.*

Micah's Mother
Judges 17

Introduction

Micah means "one who is like the Lord." As you read the text, Judges 17, see if Micah or his mother live up to such a name. So much is unknown about this lady; one way to do this study is just raise questions.

Where Did Micah's Mother Get the Money

The story begins with Micah's mother (another unnamed woman in Judges) cursing about losing 1100 shekels of silver. Micah confessed that he took (stole) the money. He returned it. Does 1100 shekels of silver sound familiar? In the Delilah story the Philistine rulers promised her 1100 shekels of silver each for finding out the secret of Samson's strength. There were five major Philistine towns. Were there five elders? If so, did she receive 5500 shekels?

Is it possible Micah's mother is Delilah? Probably not, but who knows. Where did she get the money? As in the story of Delilah, politicians have access to the peoples' tax and have no problem in buying favors with it.

Was Micah's Mother Forgiving?

To her credit, she said she forgave Micah for steeling her money. That is a sign of a good mother. A mother's love and forgiveness may be the nearest you get to a human understanding of the grace, love and forgiveness of God.

Was Micah's Mother a Cheat?

She said she would use the 1100 shekels to have a silver idol built for Micah. She gave only 200 shekels to be used in making the idol. Did the silver smith charge 900 shekels for his work? If not, what about the remaining money?

What Influence Did Micah's Mother Have on Him?

Micah took the idol and declared himself a priest. He decided to go into the business of religion. It was small scale at first. He was a priest for a household. But then a tribe wanted him and could pay a lot more. Is that the prestige, power and possession addiction showing up again?

How does this story fit into the cycle of events, repeated over and over, in the Book of Judges? Soon the whole tribe of Dan had forgotten the God who loved them, the God of Israel.

Application to Life

Think about and discuss the influence your parents had on you.

Who else was an influence on your life?

How do you influence the lives of others around you?

Can religion be turned into a money-making business? Think of examples.

Are idols worshipped in your society? Name some.

Are you tempted to make one of the idols yours?

Discuss how easy it might be to go from small missteps to major wrongs.

Prayer: *God, deliver us from the worship of false gods.*

The Levite's Concubine
Judges 19

Introduction

The woman in this study of women in the Book of Judges shows the depth of moral decay of Israel, especially against women. "There was no king in Israel, and everyone what he saw fit" or "what was right in his own sight." A statement like this is found four times in the closing chapters of Judges (17:6; 18:1; 19:1 and 21:25).

This may be a fore warning that the people are going to ask for a king like other nations have. It could emphasize the depth of lawlessness. Of course, it could mean everyone did right in the sight of God. But not these characters. What do you think?

It is in this environment that this "woman story" takes place. What happens in chapter 19, the text for this study, triggers violence, war, deprivation that continues through to the end of the book. Read the story. The concern of this study is the unnamed concubine. She was abused, used, raped, and murdered. Then her body desecrated and used to incite civil war that took the lives of thousands, according to the text.

This is another story seldom read in church. It should be prefaced by "Reader discretion advised."

The Concubine Was Mistreated

A concubine was a secondary wife. They are mentioned often in the Hebrew Bible. Their status was much lower than a wife, though some were treated with respect.

Her owner, in the story, was a Levite. He had a priestly job, high on the social scale. So immediately you see the wide class contrast between the two.

From the beginning of the story she was abused and ran away to her father's house. The Levite went to bring her back.

The Concubine is Raped and Murdered

The Levite and the concubine's father seem to have a week-long party before the Levite, his servant and his concubine began their journey home. It seems they left late in the day but found what they thought was a safe town.

A farmer returning from the fields saw them on the town square and invited them to stay with him. A ruff bunch of men went to his door and demanded, "Bring out the man who came to your house so we can have sex with him" verse 22. The man protested and offered his virgin daughter and the concubine. Who gave the concubine to them, the host or the husband Levite? Either way there seems to have been no protest from the other. Pure cowardice by both men. The virgin daughter was spared?

The Concubine's Body Was Used to Begin War

After a night of abuse and violation by what some call gang rape the concubine was found at the door of the host.

Was she dead at that point? It seems unclear.

She is taken by the Levite to his home. Whenever she died, the Levite cut her body into twelve parts and sent a part to the tribes of Israel. He called for all to participate in civil war against the tribe of Benjamin.

The rape and murder were done by some outlaws from one town, but revenge was taken out on and destroyed nearly a whole tribe. An accurate picture of the way war is, don't you think?

Application to Life

Be thankful the Bible is so truthful about the humanness of mankind. Many of the praises and problems seen in this and the other studies of women in Judges are relevant today in any society. This last study cries out how abuse of women (or men) can lead to violence, revenge, war and all kinds of bad can escalate. Take time to think about and discuss these issues. Review the previous studies.

Prayer: *Lord deliver us from evil.*

Four Hundred Virgins and Two Hundred Dancing Girls
Judges 17 – 21

Almost one fourth of the Book of Judges is given to the stories of a levite named Micah and the horrific results of his unjust, violent, and self-centered decision making. The stories are found in chapters seventeen through twenty-one. This is the same levite Micah who in the last study chopped up this concubine. One man's foolish acts ignited a whole nation's violence and civil war.

To grasp these stories, read the chapters in one sitting. In fact, it may require at least two readings to get all the tribes, towns, and persons clearly in your mind. It may help if you use a map showing the towns and each tribe's territory during the time of the Judges. Most of the towns or villages in the stories are in a line from Bethlehem in the tribe of Benjamin in the south to Shiloh to the north.

Briefly, incited by the act of Micah cutting his concubine's body into twelve parts and sending a part to each tribe; with a message that his concubine's rape and murder should not have happened in Israel or the criminals go unpunished.

So, word goes out to all the tribes to gather and demand that the guilty men be turned over to them. When that failed, they plotted to destroy the whole town of Gibeah; and then the whole tribe of Benjamin. Scores of innocent people and hundreds of fighting men on both sides died.

So many men of the tribe of Benjamin were killed, that only 600 escaped. As some semblance of family cohesion began to return to the tribes, the elders of Israel realized that there were not enough women left in Benjamin for the six hundred surviving men. All the other tribes had sworn together that none of their daughters would be given in marriage to a Benjaminite.

One foolish thing leads to another. The elders take a survey to determine which town did not show up to fight. Jabesh-Gilead did not participate. So, twelve thousand, probably twelve units, were sent to destroy the inhabitants of that town. "Go put the inhabitants of Jabesh-Gilead to the sword, including the women and little ones" 21:10. This total destruction is called herem. Yet, they found four hundred virgins there. These were brought back to be given as brides to the surviving males of Benjamin. See 21:13-14. Paula M. McNutt wrote in her notations in The New Interpreters Study Bible, that those four hundred women were turned over to those men as the concubine of Micah was turned over for gangrape. One rape has been multiplied by four hundred.

There is a downhill slide of morals from Caleb giving his daughter to Othneil for winning a battle to four hundred virgins given to the men of Benjamin.

But wait, that is not all. Four hundred is not enough for six hundred. There must be some more women somewhere. The final verses of Judges tell of a festival in Shiloh. There would be many dancing girls there. Why not send the remaining womanless men to the festival. Hide out, watch the dancing and then, kidnap the girl of your choice. Problem solved. For the fourth time the writer reminds the reader in closing the book; "In those days there was no king in Israel; all the people did what was right in their own eyes' 21:25. Could that mean what is right in the eyes of the males?

Application to Life

Those were uncivilized folk, don't you think? That could not happen in our advanced society. But it does!

Why not have someone from your local law enforcement and/or district attorney office to visit your group and enlightened you on what is happening in your community. You may be surprised what is happening to women where you live.

Find out what organizations near you are dedicated to assisting abused women. Check out *Sojourners* magazine on your computer. It will have this kind of information.

Observe the news for a week and note related articles.

Naomi
Book of Ruth

Though not included in the Book of Judges, three other women, who lived in the time of the judges of Israel, demand our attention. These three are Naomi, Ruth and Hannah. They will give us a much better feeling for those changing times. They are like salt to a bland meal; like light in the darkness.

As in all horrific and dark times, there are so many good people seeking to please God and help their fellow human beings and care for God's creation. But, then as now, the bad side gets the publicity.

These three ladies show us how God is at work in the worst of times. They give credence to Paul's words that God works in all things for good to those who love him. See Romans 8:28.

Naomi means pleasant. Her life seemed to be anything but pleasant. She, her husband and two sons move from Bethlehem to Moab, because there was famine in their area. That would be like, well, think of the place to which you would least like to move, outside your own country. There you go, not even a pleasant thought. The two sons marry women outside their faith; think on that one. Then her husband and both sons die. How bad can life get for a lady whose name means pleasant?

Naomi decides to go back home to Bethlehem. Both daughters in law offer to go with her. Think about why Naomi may have insisted they not go with her.

They would be going to a strange land where they may not be accepted. Bad things can happen to aliens. Consider what is in your news about that.

Ruth persists and goes home with Naomi. The town folk see a different person than the Naomi they had known. In fact, Naomi asked them to change their name for her to Mara, which means bitter. Ruth volunteered to join the poor in following reapers to gather the grain missed by the reapers. Let us save that story for later. Suffice to say the story of Naomi ends with her being a joyful and pleasant Grandmother. In fact, she was the Great, Great Grandmother of King David.

Application to Life

Having read the Book of Ruth, you may have some difficulty keeping Ruth separated from Naomi. The object of this study is to see and seek to emulate the wonderful character traits of Naomi; and to discuss how you and your group can minister to persons who are in grief and are aliens and those returning home, such as soldiers from war or prisoners from prison. So, think about these things by yourself, or with your group.

List the characteristics you see in Naomi that are needed in your life. What about patience, willing to change locations, concern for the daughters in law.

You do the thinking. Check your list against the love described in I Corinthians 13.

Check on organizations that are committed to assisting those in need. Where should you or your group volunteer to help?

List the persons in your area who like Naomi need comfort, help of various kinds and just acceptance and love. Decide what you can commit yourself or you group to do.

Prayer: *Lord, Help us to be sensitive to the needs of others.*

Ruth
Book of Ruth

The story of Ruth is one of the most famous and delightful stories in the Bible. Ruth is the daughter in law of Naomi, and widow of one of Naomi's sons. When Naomi decides to leave Moab and return to her home in Bethlehem, Ruth insists that she will go with her. Her words to Naomi are beautiful. Reread them, Ruth 1:16-17. Where have you heard those words? Was it at a wedding? I think it rather humorous that these are words from a daughter in law to her mother in law. Maybe the bride and groom should say them to each other and to their mothers in law at the wedding.

That was some commitment Ruth made. Where ever you go, where ever you stay, whoever your God, I'm with you to the end. So, the story has two poor widows, one old, one young, going to continue life together.

Ruth volunteers to follow the Hebrew poor women who gather the missed and dropped grain in the field. It happens that the field chosen is that of Boaz, a well to do relative of Naomi. The love story is what it is. Do not try to read your taboos and morals into it. Enjoy the story. It amounts to a beautiful young lady offering herself in marriage to a farmer in a hay stack. Was the whole episode directed by her mother in law?

You may enjoy reading the novel, *RUTH: The Woman Who Found Romance in A Barley Field*, by Vone B. Elkins. Or, use your imagination and write your own version of the love story.

The conclusion of the matter is that Ruth married Boaz; married and had a boy baby, whom the neighborhood women named Obed. Obed means worshipper. It may be short for Obadiah, worshipper of the Lord. Grandmother Naomi was his nurse and Obed became the Grandfather of King David. What a story!

Application to Life

Do you know someone like Ruth: a foreigner, widow and poor?

How would you describe her?

What do you think that person needs?

Can you or your group help?

What group or organization in your community offers help to such people?

Should you volunteer?

What do you think of persons who marry outside their race or religion?

Are they accepted in your home, group and church?

Do these ladies need child care help?

Do they need to learn child care and homemaking skills?

Do they need job skills and a job? What is your community and church doing to help?

It is interesting how the neighborhood women named the child, not his father, mother or even grandmother. Why not think about and discuss those neighborhood women in the time of Judges. What all do you think they did for Ruth and Naomi? There is another story.

Prayer: *Lord, Help us to be good neighbors.*

Hannah
I Samuel 1:1-28

With Hannah we reach the crescendo of the women of Judges. Her story is in the first and second chapters of I Samuel. She was a barren wife who prayed earnestly for a boy baby. She had a son and gave him to the Lord. She gave him with a song on her lips and in her heart. The story is short but is a high light in the Old Testament as you know or shall see.

As the story goes, Hannah was the wife of Elkhanah, who had two wives. One bore children and Hannah could not. This led to uncalled for comments and action by Pinnia; thus, adding insult to an already heartbroken Hannah. This kind of story is often repeated in Scripture. Remember or read the stories of Sarah and Hagar in Genesis chapters 16 and 21; Rebekah 25:21, Isaac married her when he was 40 and the twins were born 20 years later; Rachael and Leah in Genesis chapters 29 and 30. Elkhannah tried to comfort her by asking if his love was not better than ten sons. The obvious unrecorded answer is a resounding no. The greatest desire of a Hebrew woman seemed to be, to bear a male child.

Hannah does what she can, she prays. Even that is misinterpreted by the old priest Eli. He thinks her soundless, moving lips mean that she is drunk. He does listen to her protest and assures her that her prayer will be answered.

The following year the promised boy baby is born, and she names him Samuel (God hears). Her promise was to give him to the Lord. She seemed to make a nazirite vow for herself and the child. A portion of the vow is to not drink strong drink. It is stated that she kept that vow. Interesting that, even today, pregnant women are told not to drink strong drink. She stayed home with the baby until he was weaned. Was that four or five years? Surely old enough for the old priest and his crew to take care of and teach the lad.

When she does take him to the temple and dedicate him to the Lord. She does so with one of the most beautiful songs in the Old Testament. The Magnificat, song of Mary in Luke 1:28-38 is very similar. They both are about God, who can and will turn race, class, economics, and government systems upside down.

Her love and loyalty continued over the years. She continued returning each year and brought new clothing for the growing Samuel. Do you think she might have brought food and toys? Imagine what all they might have talked about on those visits. There is so much the Bible does not tell us.

Application to Life

Think about what you desire more than anything else in life. If it was given to you could, would you be willing to give it back to God?

Compare I Samuel 2:26 to Luke 2:52. How do you think Hannah helped with Samuels's growth?

What are you doing to grow like Samuel and Jesus?

How can you help parents, your church and society to realize the importance of early childhood education?

Only mothers know the extent of emotion at being separated from their children. Do you know mothers that need your help when their child goes away from home for work, school, and military service?

What can you, your group or your church do for those families?

Do you think there were priests' wives or other women who helped Samuel with his life of separation from his family?

Discuss prayer and waiting on God. What has been your experience?

Discuss the problems faced by childless parents who wish to have children.

Are there things that you might do to help them cope?

Prayer: *Lord, Give us grace to be gracious and generous with your gifts to us.*

www.ingramcontent.com/pod-product-compliance
Lightning Source LLC
Chambersburg PA
CBHW052206110526
44591CB00012B/2100